20

The Good Food Guide:
A Handbook For
Healthy Eating

By

Patricia A. Negron

authorHOUSE™

1663 LIBERTY DRIVE, SUITE 200
BLOOMINGTON, INDIANA 47403
(800) 839-8640
WWW.AUTHORHOUSE.COM

First published by AuthorHouse 09/03/04

ISBN: 1-4184-8237-4 (sc)

Printed in the United States of America
Bloomington, Indiana

This book is printed on acid-free paper.

Table of Contents

A Few Words About This Book

This book started as my attempt to organize the overwhelming, and often contradictory, information available from traditional sources today on what foods are good for us. Confused and irritated by the lack of clarity on even the most basic matters regarding food, I set out to find it for myself. In the process, I happily realized that with the advent of the Internet and *Google* searches, consumers are empowered to an extent that would otherwise have been impossible even just a few years ago.

I was truly amazed at the depth and breadth of relevant information now available within seconds on even the most unusual subjects. I was also surprised at the degree of consensus that I found among *bona fide* experts in academia, science and medicine on matters of considerable importance to the average person. Interestingly, the answers I got to my questions often refuted what I had been told (or not told) by my family's healthcare providers. But the most incredible discovery I made was that much of what we are "learning" today about nutrition was discovered more than 60 years ago by pioneering doctors perplexed by the onslaught of maladies among "modern" cultures early in the 20th century.

Today it is possible to review research that was previously available only to our doctors. Research that, I believe, they are no longer able to follow being so overwhelmed by a dysfunctional and backwards healthcare system. It is also now possible to call regulatory agencies to task on matters, which were previously kept out of the public eye. Matters that deeply affect consumers' well-being, yet have been politicized beyond recognition. Until I saw it for myself,

I believed, like many others of us, that somehow those entrusted with safeguarding our health were managing to do the right thing in spite of the obstacles. Unfortunately, what I found was quite the opposite.

We are only just beginning to hear about the dangers of hydrogenated oils and refined foods, which have been around since the turn of the 20th century. More recently, high fructose corn syrup, cheap vegetable oils and various food processing practices have been introduced into the mix, which also wreak havoc on our bodies. Somewhere along the line, the idea of progress has become synonymous with processed food lining our grocery store shelves and a fast food restaurant on every corner. In his widely acclaimed best seller *Fast Food Nation*, Eric Schlosser reported that by the turn of the 21st century, Americans were spending more on fast food than higher education.

Exacerbating this problem is that as urban life expanded during the 20th century, traditions in food preparation were abandoned as they became increasingly associated with peasant foods and poverty. Most of us don't have the time to spend hours every day slow cooking meats or preparing healthful broths. The reality is, however, that many of the foods that our parents and grandparents used to prepare for us, rich in organ meats (remember the liver and onions?), and animal protein and fats, were the right foods for us. Ones that we are now advised to limit by the so-called experts. While this advice is partly correct, it is so only because contamination from hormones, antibiotics and unnatural feed (along with the chemical fertilizers used to grow it), has rendered the food unfit for human consumption.

I hope you will find this book to be a thoughtful consolidation and presentation of overwhelming evidence that the quality of our food supply has deteriorated to such an extent that we are literally eating ourselves sick. I don't pretend to be an expert in molecular biology, but I did find reports from highly regarded experts in their fields and endeavored to present their findings in a way that makes sense to we regular people who just want to do what is best for our families. So in the interest of brevity, this book is not intended to be an exhaustive review of research on the quality of our current food supply. And certainly, there are relevant topics that I do not cover. However, there are a number of thorough texts and studies to which I do make reference and you should certainly peruse yourself, as you are able (most especially, Dr. Weston Price's *Nutrition and Physical Degeneration*). My objective is to educate the reader on the exceedingly low quality of the most popular foods, but then identify good food sources for making healthy choices without disrupting one's life unnecessarily - suggestions that I hope are more practical than most advice.

There are, in truth, some basic principles to follow in making good food choices; none of which include how to follow the food pyramid guidelines for eating which are, themselves, highly flawed. Another truism is that we have to recognize the limitations of our healthcare providers and how much guidance they can provide with respect to food. We have all been told to eat right and exercise. But exactly what that means is still a mystery to most of us. It is also true, I have found, that eating well is as much an art as it is a science, and takes a serious commitment to understanding why certain foods are good for us and why it is important that we endeavor to have them. The bottom line is that achieving and maintaining a state of wellness is incumbent upon each of us as individuals. And eating to be well is the best start we can make in that respect.

Bon Appetit!

The Land of Plenty

Today, in America, we congratulate ourselves for enjoying what we believe to be abundance and good fortune. We live relatively long lives, food is inexpensive and plentiful and resources of every imaginable kind are available to us on every corner. Certainly we are the envy of all our world neighbors – or are we?

While we no longer fall ill from the deadly effects of smallpox – or even the inconvenience of chicken pox, for that matter – we are grotesquely obese, and suffering from all manner of autoimmune disorders and degenerative disease. Diabetes, heart disease, asthma, autism, infertility and allergies have reached epidemic proportions. Yet we continue to demand drugs to treat the symptoms of these illnesses without stopping to consider their underlying causes – many of which are as plain as the type on our food labels.

Meanwhile, we shuttle our kids from one activity to another all the while feeding them an abundance of processed food that yields nominal nutritional value and contains excessive sweeteners, fillers and trans fats without even realizing it. Yet the experts continue to tell us that as long as we follow the food pyramid guidelines, our diets are healthy. They also have argued repeatedly that organic food is no healthier than conventionally processed food. That's interesting . . . food made without pesticides, chemical preservatives, dyes, and hormones that is also missing those key ingredients, partially hydrogenated oil and high fructose corn syrup, is not considered "healthier". Which standard would they be applying? I am afraid I am not familiar with it.

Furthermore, the FDA has failed us miserably in favoring the interests of large business. Today, produce, meats and dairy products continue to be farmed with casual disregard to the cumulative effects of pesticides, feed fertilizers, hormones and antibiotics. **Our children are being exposed to these toxic substances every time they consume a food or drink, yet the FDA has only just begun to require safety data of any kind with respect to kids in the last year. This is despite legislation in 1998 demanding it.** In fact, the Environmental Working Group found an average of 2.4 pesticides present in commercially grown apples as part of its analysis of over 100,000 tests for pesticides on fresh produce, conducted from 1992 - 2001 by the U.S. Department of Agriculture and the FDA (see www.foodnews.org). According to Environmental Working Group's February 25, 1999 report *How 'Bout Them Apples*,

- More than a quarter million American children ages one through five ingest a combination of 20 different pesticides every day. More than 1 million preschoolers eat at least 15 pesticides on a given day. Overall, 20 million American children five and under eat an average of eight pesticides every day.

- Every day, 610,000 children ages one through five -- equal to all the kids of that age in the states of Washington and Oregon combined -- consume a dose of neurotoxic organophosphate insecticides (OPs) *that the government deems unsafe*.

Some of you may recall in 1989 the consumer uproar regarding continued use of the pesticide Alar on apples in spite of data from governmental scientists that identified it as a potent carcinogen. Well, it is certainly not an isolated incident and is simply indicative of a willingness among governmental agencies to bend under industry pressure. It was only a result of consumer pressure that its use was discontinued. It is also true that many other necessary changes in the way food is currently grown and processed will only occur by way of consumer demand, not regulatory agency initiative.

The current path of modern food processing and consumption is truly unsustainable. Our health is deteriorating at an alarming rate, sapping valuable resources from productive activities to pay for the exorbitant costs of treating our litany of health issues. **A 2001 Surgeon General report noted illness from obesity alone cost the United States $117 billion the previous year.** We are literally eating ourselves sick and then gratefully accepting conventional medical treatment that really does nothing to address the causes of our illnesses. With every successive generation, we are becoming sicker and fatter.

And while the quality of our food supply alone does not fully explain the high rate of illness among Americans, it certainly goes a long way to doing so. Garbage in, garbage out. Our bodies are literally *made* from what we eat. And they are only as good as the materials we provide for building them. If you consider how rampant birth defects, disease and learning disabilities are among our youngest generation today, we can only imagine what the next generation will face. The healthy child - free of disabilities, allergies and chronic illness - is rapidly becoming the exception rather than the rule. The first step toward reversing this trend is having a high quality food supply. In addition, by demanding changes in current food processing practices, we will eliminate many environmental contaminants, which also contribute to the deterioration of our health.

In those rapidly vanishing native peoples whose food supply has not yet been contaminated and diet has remained essentially unchanged for many thousands of years, one will find consistently healthy, happy individuals who reproduce with ease. Yet how could it be that "primitive" cultures, subsisting on large amounts of animal fats and organ meats raised on a natural diet, need none of our miracle drugs to thrive and reproduce? They eat properly from high quality food sources.

As far back as the 1930s, Dr. Weston Price conducted landmark research on the ill effects of the "modern" diet and found that poor dental health was a symptom of poor general health caused by a bad diet. He found that **within the span of a *single generation*, the introduction of processed foods to a pregnant mother's diet commonly resulted in children with narrow dental arches, crooked teeth and decay.** The beaming smiles and optimism of their parents were gone. Moreover, these children suffered all manner of general health issues and infections their parents had never known. In fact, he found that within single communities those individuals who adopted modern diets suffered frequently from tuberculosis. Unbelievably, tuberculosis was absent among those living in the *same* community who maintained a traditional diet. He was not alone in his observations and today, science has reinforced his findings with new studies showing that if a pregnant woman eats a high carbohydrate diet, the fetus will become more insulin resistant. Moreover, if the fetus is female, her eggs will be more insulin resistant.

What follows is my own small effort to educate consumers in a way that empowers them to protect their health and well-being in the most basic sense possible: by eating to be well. There is no doubt that food raised and processed properly is more expensive compared to its cheap counterparts. However, when you add up the true costs of the cheap alternatives by including the damage they do to our health, lost productivity due to illness and expensive medications (be they prescription or over-the-counter), expensive dental work as well as environmental damage, you will find that the high quality food is a much better value.

Feel Ill? Take a Pill!

I was listening to one of the national morning programs the other day, and one topic of discussion was that heart disease has become the number one killer among women. A well-known physician was lending his expertise in helping viewers understand their options for treatment and prevention. He reviewed the most effective medications currently available for treating the disease and then ran through the usual laundry list of preventive measures that people can take: eat well, exercise, reduce stress and get plenty of rest.

While I have enormous respect for this particular individual, I was especially disturbed by his emphasis on treating an already existing condition with medications that reduce symptoms and do nothing to resolve the heart disease. Its practical application is akin to prescribing a decongestant to someone with the sniffles and claiming to have cured the common cold. I think it drove home to me the fundamental problem with how we approach wellness in a way that I had never fully appreciated until that day.

Today, we are facing a national crisis with respect to affordable prescription medication. **According to the Center for Financing, the number of outpatient medications utilized by Americans age 65 and older in the year 2000 was *23* on average with out-of-pocket expenditures of \$623.** Among those under 65, it was still a whopping *ten* prescriptions with average out-of-pocket expenditures of \$200. Total expenditures increased by more than 40% from \$72 billion to \$103 billion in just four years.

According to the American Heart Association (AHA), coronary heart disease killed more than 500,000 Americans in 2001, the most recently available data. More than 1.6 million patients discharged from hospitals that year were diagnosed with heart disease. This data is for a *single* year. The AHA also reported that cardiovascular disease is the *number 3* killer among children under the age of 15. I don't know about you, but I find this last statistic truly shocking.

While about 30% of the deaths from heart disease among adults are attributed to smoking, by virtual consensus, the majority can be attributed to trans fats (i.e. partially hydrogenated vegetable oils) in our diets. The FDA itself acknowledges that trans fats are a major culprit, yet the agency has taken four years to act on legislation requiring the labeling of trans fats and will allow three more to pass before implementing the requirement.

Similar to the effects of smoking tobacco, people don't usually drop dead instantaneously from eating trans fats. In most cases, it takes many years for the most devastating effects to be realized. Not unlike partially hydrogenated vegetable oils, tobacco plays no useful role in our lives. And for more than 40 years, it has been well understood that trans fats cause heart disease. Yet, the maxim "eat well" still gets nothing more than lip service by those whom we trust most to advise us on how to stay healthy. One reason may be is that there is much less money to be made by keeping people well as opposed to treating them with expensive prescription medications and procedures once they are ill.

The worst part of it all is that when it comes to hydrogenated oils/trans fats, the real victims are not consenting adults who choose to accept responsibility for risky behavior (i.e. smoking). They are the children of unwitting parents who are feeding them what they believe to be nutritious foods. The fact of the matter, however, is that with nearly every single meal that most children eat, they are also ingesting potentially deadly trans fats. Trans fats are everywhere and they are insidious. As you go down the grocery store isles you will find them in all of the most popular brand name foods, especially those targeted to children. Trans fats are in brand name graham crackers, cheese crackers, frozen chicken tenders, cereal, cookies, muffins, bagels, cereal bars and even multi-grain bread.

Trans fats kill thousands of people each year in the form of heart disease developed from years of consuming them just as smoking cigarettes kills people after a lifetime of indulgence. The difference is that the FDA has failed to either protect or inform us, and our children are the victims of their negligence.

Another challenge that consumers face, is avoiding the exorbitant amounts of high fructose corn syrup (HFCS) in virtually every conventionally processed food available on grocery store shelves and in restaurants. **HFCS does not trigger our bodies to produce insulin and, in fact, fructose inhibits the body's ability to maintain proper insulin blood levels.** Everything from refined white sugar to naturally occurring sugar in maple syrup causes our bodies to produce insulin in its presence, which allows the sugar to be converted to energy. In addition, these sugars also known as sucrose and glucose, cause a hormonal reaction that tells us when we are full. Not so with HFCS. As a result, when we consume it, we are being overloaded with a substance that our bodies simply cannot process. Our systems are being flooded with artificial sugars that are not digested properly and damage our health. But we never hear a word about the dangers HFCS from our healthcare providers or the FDA.

Yet in April 2004, *Yahoo News* reported that in 2001, an estimated 16 million Americans were living with type 2 diabetes attributed to smoking and cheap food. That number is expected to rise to 29 million by the year 2050. It is also known that nearly two-thirds of diabetics develop heart disease. Insulin resistance, which is related to lipid (cholesterol) imbalances, increases triglycerides.

Adding insult to injury, the U.S. federal government continues to administer policy that encourages farmers to raise too much corn, the main ingredient in HFCS. As a result, food companies use the cheap substance in their products to make easy prey of children for their poor quality foods. Meanwhile, the economics of capitalism encourages the healthcare industry to create recurring sources of revenue such as those that treat symptoms not prevent or cure disease.

One challenge is to change our perspective from a "silver bullet" mentality and recognize that whole foods are more valuable than their individual parts. For example, while calcium is necessary for strong bones, it is useless without magnesium and vitamin D, or the presence of saturated fat and enzymes needed to absorb it. As a result, supplementation and fortification alone are simply not the answer. Unfortunately, however, our soil has been so depleted of its mineral content by modern farming practices that most of us will require at least some supplementation even on the most healthful of diets.

The bottom line is that Americans don't need a prescription drug plan, they need a better food supply.

The Flawed Food Pyramid

The basic truth is that doctors are trained in the practice of medicine, not nutrition. They spend their years of training learning to diagnose health conditions, prescribe medications and perform medical procedures, not recommend a nutritious diet. Thus, they rely upon misleading industry information that tells us to eat lots of grains and to minimize our intake of animal fats. Ask your physician about HFCS or hydrogenated oils. Then do a *Google* search on your own and see how closely the information correlates to your doctor's advice. If, by chance, it does, you are probably going to be left wondering why you weren't warned against consuming these substances long before. After all, the vast majority of us rely primarily on our healthcare providers to guide us on good nutrition and keep us well.

If we just apply good common sense, we can see that only in the last century heart disease has become a major issue even as Americans have cut far back on their animal fat consumption and substituted vegetable fats. Remember those big containers of vegetable shortening in your parent's and grandparent's kitchens? For so many thousands of years, people have consumed animals and their fats in much higher proportion than they consumed grains, and thrived. Still, we are consistently guided by "professionals" to reduce our intake of animal fats and substitute them with vegetable oils. Even as we get exorbitantly fatter and sicker.

Furthermore, even as Americans have cut back significantly on their sugar consumption during the last 30 years, their intake of HFCS has exploded. It should be no surprise that **according to the National Institutes of Health, diabetes was the cause of nearly *twenty percent* of all deaths among those 25 years and older in the U.S. during 1999.**

11

It is believed that more than six percent of the population has diabetes and that every year there are one million new cases.

So, I'm no rocket scientist, but I am having a really hard time understanding the current so-called wisdom on nutrition. Especially when the infamous food pyramid defies what history so clearly tells us and completely overlooks the realities of today's food processing practices. But don't take my word for it. See for yourself. There is a growing body of literature by disinterested parties including Dr. Walter C. Willett, Chairman of the Department of Nutrition at the Harvard School of Public Health and Professor of Medicine at the Harvard Medical School. He is generally recognized as one of the world's top authorities on nutrition and calls the partial hydrogenation of oils the "biggest food-processing disaster in U.S. history". **Dr. Willett estimates that trans fats cause as many as 100,000 premature coronary deaths every year.**

Prima facie, there are a number of major problems with the food pyramid approach:

A Conflict of Interest
The food pyramid was co-developed in 1992 by the U.S. Department of Agriculture (USDA), which is responsible for overseeing the production of wheat and corn in the United States. Both are heavily subsidized with federal funds with direct government payments of cash topping $20 billion for U.S. farmers in 1999. Meanwhile, U.S. farm policy has flooded world markets with the commodities and driven down prices for the crops to levels that make it impossible to realize a profit. With the passage of the Farm Bill in 1996, prices plummeted 40% within five years, the lowest level seen in more than a decade.

As a result, the industry has been desperate to find markets for its product. Corn is not only the chief crop consumed by humans in a multitude of forms including HFCS and regular corn syrup, it is so cheap that it is fed to livestock and poultry for which it is an unnatural diet. In both cases, it has produced disastrous results. Yet the farmers keep producing it, and we keep subsidizing it. Now they want to further expand their production capacity by using Genetically Modified Organisms (GMOs), which have been declared "safe" by the FDA in the absence of sufficient data to support its position. In fact, a U.S. District Court judge found in September 2000 that the FDA ignored its scientific staff's concerns regarding the safety of GMOs, that they are not being regulated, and that there is significant disagreement among scientific experts regarding their safety. Unfortunately, the judge's ruling favored the FDA's position on technical grounds. For details, visit www.biointegrity.org

Grains are the Foundation of a Good Diet
Upon his return from conducting extensive global research in 1990, Dr. Vernon Young, a professor of nutritional biology at MIT for 40 years, concluded that adults need two to three times the daily protein recommended by the World Health Organization and two United Nations organizations at that time. This was two years prior to the development of the U.S. Food Pyramid. There is little to no historical evidence to support the contention that grains are the foundation for a "well-balanced" diet. Dr. Loren Cordain, a renowned expert in the Paleolithic (a.k.a. Stone Age) diet and professor of exercise physiology at Colorado State University, together with Dr. Walter Willett of the Harvard School of Public Health, have publicly criticized this recommendation. Both point to the recent advent of the grinding stone (in evolutionary terms) and a lack of

empirical evidence to suggest that a diet high in complex carbohydrates promotes good health. Specifically, Dr. Cordain found that:

> [t]he fossil record indicates that early farmers, compared to their hunter-gatherer predecessors had a characteristic reduction in stature, an increase in infant mortality, a reduction in life span, an increased incidence of infectious diseases, an increase in iron deficiency anemia, an increased incidence of osteomalacia, porotic hyperostosis and other bone mineral disorders and an increase in the number of dental caries and enamel defects.

Furthermore, upon examining recently compiled ethnographic data from 181 worldwide societies of hunter-gatherers, Dr. Cordain found that the mean plant to animal subsistence ratio in terms of energy was **35% plant** and **65% animal**. To be clear, the 35% in the plant category means fruits and vegetables, not grains. Interestingly, Dr. Cordain has found that epidemiological studies of populations consuming high levels of unleavened whole grain breads show vitamin D deficiency to be widespread, with the incidence of rickets on the rise.

A medical rarity at the beginning of the twentieth century, within 50 years heart disease would become America's number one killer. Today, heart disease causes at least 40% of all deaths in the United States. Meanwhile, between 1910 and 1970 consumption of animal fat reportedly declined from 83% to 62% of the average American diet. Interestingly, butter consumption also declined during that period from eighteen pounds per year to four pounds. Even among "modern" cultures in France, Italy and Greece where traditional diets persist, you will find generous amounts of meat and/or dairy products at every meal yet a dramatically lower incidence of heart disease relative to Americans.

Another perspective on the importance of fat and cholesterol in our diet is to note that breastmilk has more cholesterol than almost any other food with more than 50% of its calories from saturated fat in early lactation. That is because cholesterol and saturated fat are absolutely critical to proper brain development in children. Yet, not only do our pediatricians fail to inform parents that these two components are virtually absent in commercial formula, they routinely recommended reduced fat dairy products for our children beginning at one year of age.

Some would also have you believe that a predominantly vegetarian diet is preferable for nursing mothers to reduce their infant's exposure to chemicals, hormones and pesticides. However, the answer is to find *organic* sources of animal fat. Nursing mothers must have ample animal fat to produce large amounts of high quality breastmilk. The problem is with industry practices that produce the contaminants, not the breastmilk. That is not to say that individuals who choose to avoid animal products cannot achieve reasonably good health. The reality is, however, that the best diet possible for realizing our highest human potential is one that consists of generous amounts of animal products.

The "Enriched" Fallacy
The food pyramid makes no distinction regarding the quality of various grains it so strongly urges us to eat. We see "enriched flour" on a food label and envision vast fields of whole grains that are then processed to make them even better than if they were used just the way they are. The truth of the matter, however, is that modern agricultural

15

practices strip the soil of its nutrients, thus destroying the quality of the crops grown in it. Then, most of those paltry nutrients are removed during processing, rendering the grain a simple sugar equivalent that mimics what you find in regular sweets such as candy. This is the biggest problem with today's carbohydrates. Nutrients are then added to "enrich" it making it effectively a lollipop with vitamins and minerals.

In contrast, *whole* grains (a.k.a. unbromated) provide long-lasting energy because they are complex carbohydrates not so easily converted to fat. If you review the labels on the carbohydrates in your cabinets, you will probably find that while you thought you were eating the recommended amount of grains, you are in fact eating a great deal of food made from "enriched" flours, and essentially sugar. The excess sugars then cause the liver to produce triglycerides, high levels of which have been linked to proneness to heart disease.

Silent Killers
Most processed foods contain two artificial ingredients in large portion, partially hydrogenated vegetable oil and HFCS. Both of these ingredients are highly problematic in the way they act in our bodies, but neither one is addressed on any level by those advising us on our diets. Neither of them is a naturally occurring substance. Consider the cereal bars you may have in your cabinet. It would not be unreasonable for the average consumer to assume that they provide a significant source of good nutrition. After all, they say, "Good Source of Calcium". Unfortunately, however, you will find enriched flour, HFCS and partially hydrogenated vegetable oil at the top of the ingredient list. None of these things contributes to our good health, and they are increasingly shown to detract from it.

Partially Hydrogenated Vegetable Oil

Also known as trans fats, there is an abundance of evidence (some dating back more than 50 years) that hydrogenated oils, which made their debut at the turn of the 20th century, are associated with all manner of health problems ranging from immune system dysfunction to heart disease to birth defects. The evidence has become so alarming that in 2003 Canadian Parlamentarian Pat Martin introduced legislation to ban them from the food supply altogether.

A 1997 *New England Journal of Medicine* study found that consuming *one gram* of trans fats a day for ten years produced a 20 percent increased risk of cardiovascular disease. The average American easily consumes at least *eight to ten* grams of trans fats per day.

Some examples of trans fats in our diet include:

Table: Trans Fats in Common Foods

Food	Trans fats (g)/serving
Fries (Medium)	14.5
Doughnut	5
Potato chips (sm. bag)	3.2
Pound cake	4.3

Source: University of Pennsylvania

If you believe that trans fats are not a problem for you because your family does not eat the items listed above with great regularity, you are not alone. Choosy moms choose a popular brand of peanut butter, right? Many consider peanut butter to be a healthy source of protein. Well, think again. Most conventionally produced peanut butter contains partially hydrogenated vegetable oil and several grams of trans fats per serving.

Varying but significant amounts of trans fats are also present in all the most popular brands of breads, fresh baked muffins and pastries, pizza, sandwich rolls, chicken tenders, frozen waffles, cheese crackers, packaged cheese, dry cereal, oatmeal, animal crackers, cereal bars, toaster pastries, pancake mixes, cake mixes, microwave popcorn and much more. Don't be fooled by clever marketing. Be sure to read the labels on everything you buy. Even "gourmet" bakeries use them, so never assume that "high quality" is synonymous with not having anything deleterious to your health. It's purely marketing hype in today's world.

I also don't think it is any accident that foods containing partially hydrogenated oils seem to be incredibly addictive. I have personally found myself craving such foods to an unusual degree. It would only take having some on a single occasion and I would find myself going back for more with alarming frequency. While I am not suggesting that the use of hydrogenated oils is some sort of conspiracy, I also don't think it is lost on the food companies that the ingredient tends to keep consumers coming back for more even against their better judgment.

Dr. Andrew Weil, a nationally recognized expert on health, has long been a proponent of eliminating hydrogenated oils from the diet. And for good reason. Trans fats increase harmful LDL cholesterol and decrease good HDL cholesterol. Saturated fats from animals, on the other hand, *increase* good HDL cholesterol. While they also increase harmful LDL cholesterol when consumed in excess, saturated fats are essential for proper cellular and heart function, as well as hormonal balance. Furthermore, as far back as the 1940s, research on hydrogenated fats linked them to cancer. Unfortunately, they were still being lumped together with saturated fats and thus began the false notion that the culprit was animal fat.

In order to hydrogenate oils, commercial processing uses high heat and chemicals to extract oils from grain by pressure followed by soaking in chemical solvents. They are then degummed, refined, bleached, and deodorized using steam distillation, which heats oils to 464 degrees to 518 degrees and destroys any remaining nutrients.

When heated to temperatures above 302 degrees, unsaturated fatty acids become mutagenic, which means they can damage our genes (and those of our offspring). Further damage occurs at higher temperatures. When oils are heated to 320 degrees, trans-fatty acids begin to form. The higher the temperature, the more trans-fatty acids form.

High heat (in excess of 320 degrees) changes the molecular configuration of unsaturated oil. In its original molecular configuration, it fits perfectly into enzyme and membrane structures. A trans-fatty acid, only slightly different in its structure, only half fits into those same enzymes and membranes. In this partial fit, it cannot do the work of a normal fatty acid and, at the same time, it blocks the pathway of the normal fatty acids.

Among the problems caused by trans-fatty acids is that they impair the protective barrier around cells, which is essential for keeping cells alive and healthy. Food must be assimilated in some way to function essentially as raw material for new cell growth: tissue, blood, organs, and hormones that ebb and flow throughout our bodies. In fact, when we ingest trans fats, our bodies mistake them for saturated fats and incorporate them into our cell membranes. As a result, the cells become vulnerable to deterioration, and at the same time they can lose important molecular components necessary for proper function. It is also likely that trans-fatty acids affect heart function, because the heart is fueled by fatty acids (another reason to ensure adequate saturated fat intake).

Despite the fact that it has been widely reported for years that trans fats are an insidious dietary problem for Americans, it took the FDA until July 2003 to act on a 1999 proposal to list them separately on food labels. The agency long argued that to do so would confuse the consumer. Some argued that to alert consumers of the dangers of trans fats would drive them to choose supposedly harmful saturated fats in their stead. Well, that's nice, but *saturated fats play an important and relevant role in our diets and are necessary to maintaining our good health.* Substituting them with a processed fat with absolutely *no* redeeming qualities as well as very serious negative consequences with respect to our health is clearly preferable, right?

And even the listing requirement lacks any real teeth. It requires only that trans fats be listed separately without any reference to a recommend daily allowance. Not surprisingly, **the recommended daily allowance is *zero*.** The national Academies' Institute of Medicine, a panel established to advise the FDA on trans fats, found *no* evidence that trans fats are essential to the diet. In addition, foods that contain trans fats that are below 0.5 grams per serving will not be required to list them separately. As a result, unless you carefully check the ingredient list for partially hydrogenated vegetable oil, or ask your server about its presence in food when you eat out, you are likely to be getting several grams of trans fats per day when all is said and done.

High Fructose Corn Syrup (HFCS)

Beginning in the 1970's, HFCS has become used widely in processed foods, including those that would otherwise be considered healthy such as yogurt. You can find it everywhere including fruit juice drinks, ketchup, barbeque sauce, jelly, jams, applesauce, ice cream, bread, pasta sauce and cereal bars. According to a *Today* show report by Phil Lempert, while many reports show that American consumption of white refined sugar has dropped over the past 20 years, it is mostly a result of the switch by food companies to HFCS, which according to USDA figures shows increased consumption of 250 percent over the last 15 years. Consumption of HFCS has risen from zero pounds per person in 1966 to more than 62 pounds per person in 2001. **Estimates are that we consume about twenty percent of our daily calories in the form of fructose.** This equates to a single soft drink for the average child.

Meanwhile, high fructose diets have been implicated in the development of adult-onset diabetes. **In addition to the fact that HFCS does not trigger insulin production, fructose, especially when combined with other sugars, reduces stores of chromium, a mineral essential for maintaining balanced insulin levels**, according to Richard Anderson, Ph.D., lead scientist at the Human Nutrition Research Center in Beltsville, Maryland. Researchers from the Department of Nutrition at the University of California, Davis, the U.S. Department of Agriculture Western Human Nutrition Research Center at Davis, California, the Monell Chemical Sense Institute and the University of Pennsylvania, Philadelphia, have recently published a landmark review of the scientific literature on fructose, weight gain, and the insulin resistance syndrome, popularly called Syndrome X. Coined by Gerry Reaven of Stanford University in the late 1980s, Syndrome X is a hidden but life-threatening perversion of bodily metabolism that is likely to lead to an early death. High fructose diets bombard the liver with triglycerides, which causes the muscle cells to become insulin-resistant. Over time, this then happens to the fat cells as well, which results in the destruction of pancreatic insulin-secreting cells. Insulin resistance is exacerbated by frequent meals and snacks, a popular practice among Americans, which also tax the pancreas. The result is Syndrome X.

Not surprisingly, there is growing evidence that HFCS is also a significant culprit in the rampant obesity among children. Because the sugar is not metabolized normally, it is quickly converted to fat, which our bodies would otherwise draw from during fasting periods. In addition, fructose does not trigger a normal hormonal response that tells us when we are full. As a result, we eat far more than we need. Furthermore, food is so abundant now and Americans are generally so sedentary that we are never in need of food before we have more. Given the high rates at which HFCS is consumed, it is no wonder American kids are getting bigger every year.

HFCS's proliferation is particularly disturbing in light of the fact that there are excellent *all-natural* alternatives such as stevioside, 300 times as sweet as sucrose, and used for many centuries as a sweetener. In addition to having a very long track record, it is shown to be safe for diabetics and hypoglycemics, to boot. However, despite extensive effort to gain approval for use in the U.S. food market, the FDA abruptly banned it reportedly on the request of Monsanto, the maker of NutraSweet. This was despite the complete absence of negative study data on stevioside and substantial demand from the food industry. In fact, a study done at Purdue University's Dental Science Research center found that not only is it 100% compatible with fluoride, it "significantly" *inhibits* plaque buildup and dental caries.

That's interesting, ban a completely safe, healthy natural sweetener and maintain approval on a synthetic one with no meaningful track record and a questionable degree of safety regarding long-term use. Another move by the FDA well off the mark of protecting the quality of our food supply. *Note:* stevioside is, however, available in supplement form.

An Altered Food Chain

Commercial feeding practices of meat and poultry stock, which use corn instead of a natural diet of grass and insects, have exacerbated the problem of saturated fat intake and fatty acid imbalance in our diets. **In today's red meat, you will find *twenty-five to thirty percent fat* content, more than six times that commonly found in free living or wild animals, which is typically four percent.** Furthermore, the fat content itself is altered by the unnatural feeding practices of conventionally raised animals. It contains little, if any, omega-3 fatty acids in its mostly saturated fat content. According to a 1985 article in the *New England Journal of Medicine*, free living and wild game contains at least five times more polyunsaturated fat per gram. About four percent of the fat is omega-3 fatty acids.

Another example of the effects of modern commercial feeding practices is that eggs from grain fed chickens contain as much as *nineteen* times the amount of omega-6 fatty acids as those from grass/pasture fed chickens whose diet consists mainly of grass and insects. Yes, it's true. A natural diet for chickens is grass and bugs. The same goes for meats. Grain fed animals yield high amounts of omega-6 fatty acids. A disproportionately high omega-6 intake in combination with a low intake of omega-3 fatty acids has been linked to autoimmune disorders such as asthma, as well as heart disease and learning deficiencies. In contrast, pasture fed animals have just the right mix of omega-3 and omega-6. So there is a big difference between the two.

The Saturated Fat Fallacy

We are advised that polyunsaturated oils are good for us, and saturated fats, particularly those from animals, are bad. Most of the fatty acids our grandparents grew up on were either saturated or monounsaturated, and came from butter, lard, and other animal fats. Today, those fats have been replaced by polyunsaturated ones: primarily vegetable oils, such as soy, corn, safflower and canola. Sally Fallon points out in her book *Nourishing Traditions* that **today as much as 30 percent of our calories come from polyunsaturated oil, a significant multiple of the four percent we should be getting.**

Research suggests that excess consumption of polyunsaturated oils contributes to a number of developmental problems and disorders. When they are used in cooking and processing, they become rancid with exposure to high heat. As this happens, free radicals are produced that damage DNA/RNA throughout the body, setting the stage for tumor growth and plaque buildup in the blood vessels, among other things. Another contributing factor is that polyunsaturated fats in vegetable oil have high omega-6 linoleic acid and only small amounts of omega-3 linolenic. These are necessary for the production of prostoglandins, which regulate cellular activity and control inflammation, blood pressure and immune system activity. When these become out of balance, the results are disastrous.

Overwhelming evidence gathered from analyzing the diets of native peoples around the world demonstrates an emphasis on lean animal protein, fish, shellfish, organ meats and animal fats (including milk), complemented by fruits and vegetables. Among these groups there exists no detectable degree of degenerative disease, chronic illness, birth defects, tooth decay or crowding. At the same time, these communities enjoy high fertility rates and low infant mortality in the absence of environmental contamination. Furthermore, among those evaluated, there appears to be consistent good mental health. Dr. Weston Price's *Nutrition and Physical Degeneration*, provides exhaustive data on this subject.

Mal-Nutrition Labels

The FDA came into existence in 1930 as a law enforcement agency to address deceptive practices. Later, the Federal Food, Drug and Cosmetic Act of 1938 was passed and required, among other things, that drugs be shown safe before they are approved for use. Thus the platform was established for the FDA to approve substances for human consumption. Unfortunately, in its application, the FDA's track record has been to approve substances only to ban them once a critical mass of injuries has developed or in the presence of a consumer uproar.

Consistent with its historical performance and despite the accumulation of data, the FDA resisted consumer efforts that would require food companies to list trans fats on nutrition labels until 2003. The issue was clearly not one of inadequate information. In fact, the FDA had even gone so far as to develop a set of scenarios for determining what benefits should be paid for the onset of heart disease and human life lost to heart disease resulting from non-disclosure of trans fats (Federal Register/Vol. 64, No. 221/Wednesday, November 17, 1999, Table 4 – Methods and Scenarios Used to Estimate Benefits), *four years* before acting.

The FDA itself has estimated that between 2,000 and 5,600 lives a year would be saved by trans fat *labeling* and 7,600 to 17,100 cases of coronary heart disease per year would be prevented. Still, it was not until July 2003, four years after the original proposal to do so, that the agency acted to require food companies list trans fats on their products. Of course, the requirement will not go into effect until 2006. Let's see, according to its own highly conservative estimates, that would be a total of 14,000 to 39,000 lives lost and 53,000 to 119,000 cases of heart disease as a result of the FDA's negligence. We are just talking about LABELING here! Imagine the number of lives that would be spared by *banning* trans fats.

Interestingly, Kraft Foods was the primary source of objection to the 2002 proposal by the FDA to list trans fats in a manner consistent with the requirements of the Nutrition Labeling and Education Act of 1990. Take a look at the ingredient list on the company's most famous cookie and you will see why. The good news is that under threat of lawsuit as well as significant consumer pressure, Kraft recently agreed to reformulate its Oreo cookies without partially hydrogenated oils. (I think Newman's Own taste better, anyway). In addition, Campbell Soup has agreed to eliminate partially hydrogenated oils from its entire cracker line, including its Goldfish brand of crackers, which are so popular among children.

Maybe some day, we will no longer see partially hydrogenated oil in any of the foods that we eat. But it will most certainly be the result of consumer pressure, however, and no thanks to the FDA. And who knows with what newfangled concoction food companies will replace it.

Pasteurization & Homogenization

Pasteurization is widely considered to be a revolutionary practice that protects and ensures the safety of our milk supply. In 1908, when commercial pasteurization was introduced, milking practices still lacked a sterile environment and the risk of contamination grew as milk production increased. In addition, large dairies able to afford the cost of pasteurization, found it to be an effective marketing tool for their milk. In 1938, pasteurization became an industry requirement and thus began the false notion that unpasteurized milk was somehow unsafe.

Today the milking process is highly sterile at licensed dairies. In fact, it is higher for certified raw milk than pasteurized. And in California where unpasteurized (raw) milk has always been available for commercial sale, every instance of contamination on record has been of pasteurized milk. Not one reported case was the result of ingesting raw milk.

Raw milk contains beneficial lactic-acid-producing bacteria, which naturally destroy pathogens that might otherwise contaminate it. It is the same bacteria used to culture yogurt. Successful pasteurization destroys all of these enzymes and thus destroys the milk's natural anti-bacterial properties. Refrigerated raw milk will begin to turn sour in about two weeks, but can still be safely consumed. While it might not be appetizing in a glass, it makes for frothy, delicious pancakes and other delectable treats such as *crème fraiche*. In fact, sour (a.k.a. cultured) milk is used to make yogurt, kefir, butter and cheese. The culturing process actually enhances the nutritional value of the milk. On the other hand, when pasteurized milk goes sour, it putrefies and has to be discarded. If ingested, it will cause diarrhea and other gastrointestinal disruption.

Another thing that happens during pasteurization is that heat changes the amino acids lysine and tyrosine in the milk making them more difficult to absorb. As a result, the pancreas is constantly strained to compensate, a condition that has been linked to diabetes. In fact, pasteurized milk consumption is increasingly believed to be a culprit in adult-onset diabetes. Like vegetable oils, high heat used for pasteurization causes the otherwise healthy fatty acids in milk to become rancid (creating free radicals) and destroys its important and naturally occurring vitamins such as C, D and B_{12}. In addition, its many mineral components become less available. Finally, the natural enzymes in milk that are destroyed during pasteurization are what help the body absorb its abundant vitamins and minerals. **Pasteurization makes the major part of calcium insoluble so that it can't be effectively absorbed.** Wait. Isn't that why we are supposed to drink milk in the first place? It also leaches mineral stores in our bones. You may be interested to know that while the U.S. boasts the highest per capita consumption of dairy products in the world, it also has the highest rate of bone fractures and osteoporosis.

Furthermore, **in 1983, Dr. Frank Oski, an internationally recognized specialist in childhood nutritional deficiencies and former Chairman of Pediatrics at Johns Hopkins University School of Medicine wrote *Don't Drink Your Milk* citing a laundry list of medical issues related to the consumption of pasteurized milk.** It is a leading cause of recurrent ear infections among children and has also been linked to insulin-dependent diabetes and other serious, but less common, illnesses such as rheumatoid arthritis, infertility and leukemia. Given the book's title, it is obvious that Dr. Oski strongly advised against pasteurized milk consumption, yet pediatricians continue to urge parents to serve it to their children daily. While at the time Dr. Oski did not link the problems to specific modern processing practices, many experts since him have done so.

Meanwhile, many credit synthetic vitamin D supplementation in today's milk for its wondrous ability to prevent severe vitamin D deficiency in children, also known as rickets. However, some nutrition experts believe that supplementation with fish liver oil is actually responsible for the elimination of rickets 75 years ago, not synthetic vitamin D in pasteurized milk. In addition, there is not sufficient vitamin D in pasteurized milk to meet the average American's dietary need. It contains under 100 IU per glass, less than 10% of the current recommendation of 1000 IU for individuals who receive limited exposure to sunlight (*J Intern Med* 2000; 247:260-268). Most Americans fall into that category, especially those with dark skin.

In reality, "vitamin D" is not a vitamin at all. It is a hormone that is produced in the skin and is essential for endocrine (hormonal) balance. It is also necessary to maintain healthy levels of calcium and phosphorous in the body and it occurs naturally in raw milk. **In fact, despite the continued emphasis on fortified milk as an important source of vitamin D, according to Krispin Sullivan with the Clinical Nutrition Office at the National Institutes of Health, vitamin D deficiency continues to be a significant concern among children and adults.** In addition, an article in the *Journal of Pediatrics* (August 2000; 137: 153-157) has determined that rickets is on the rise in the United States. William Grant, a leading researcher on the subject, believes the vast majority of Americans are deficient to a meaningful extent with the most severe cases among dark-skinned individuals living in Alaska and urban regions of the northeast.

While the deficiency is most closely associated with bone diseases such as osteoporosis and rickets, **insufficient vitamin D has also been linked with cancer risk, autism, insulin deficiency, multiple sclerosis, Seasonal Affective Disorder, Crohn's disease, obesity and Syndrome X**. A study published in the January 13, 2004 edition of *Neurology* indicated that women who consumed 400 IU of vitamin D daily were 40% less likely to develop multiple sclerosis. While it may seem ridiculous that even a slight deficiency in a single hormone could cause all of these problems, remember that hormonal balance is an extremely delicate matter and when even slightly askew, an imbalance can trigger a cascade of troubles.

The reality is, in fact, good ol' sunshine and a high quality food supply are the answer, not synthetic "enrichment". In his new book, *The UV Advantage*, Dr. Michael Holick, professor of Medicine and Dermatology at Boston University School of Medicine, recommends direct exposure to noontime sun without sunscreen with only fifteen to thirty minutes necessary for fair complexions and as much as several hours for those with very dark skin. Liver, dark leafy greens such as collards, kale and spinach, fatty fish and cod liver oil are excellent food sources of natural vitamin D. Unfortunately, widespread mercury and PCB contamination in freshwater and shell fish, which are otherwise nearly perfect foods, has made their regular consumption unadvisable, especially for pregnant or nursing mothers and their young children. Believe it or not, this also includes farmed fish. (*Note*: There is currently underway an effort to allow for even higher industrial discharges of mercury into the environment).

The final insult with respect to modern milk processing techniques is homogenization. Homogenization is the process by which the fat globules in milk are strained to make them smaller and keep them from separating in the milk. Otherwise, the cream floats to the top. When milk is homogenized, small fat globules surround a protein enzyme in the milk called xanthine oxidase, which is then absorbed intact into your blood stream. There is evidence demonstrating clear associations with this absorbed enzyme and increased risks of heart disease. Furthermore, there is some evidence that the resulting fat globules are changed from their original composition and form a new membrane that contains more whey proteins and casein, which might be what makes them more allergenic.

I still don't get the point of homogenization and why it is somehow desirable. All you have to do is shake the container.

Also, beware of reduced fat milk. Powdered skim milk is used in its production. The cholesterol is oxidized during the dehydration process, making it harmful to the arteries and the high temperatures used create nitrites, which are carcinogenic, and free glutamic acid (a.k.a. hydrolyzed proteins such as monosodium glutamate or MSG), to which many people are sensitive. Again, the truth is, you *need* the fat and cholesterol you get from full fat milk for good health.

Antibiotics & Hormones

Conventional U.S. farmers routinely inject our meat supply with mega doses of antibiotics because the conditions under which the animals are raised are so unhealthy. We also know that antibiotics must be metabolized by the animals and that they are not completely eliminated from the animals' systems under the best of conditions. So where do you think all of the remaining substance goes? It is stored in the fat, milk, organ and muscle tissue of the animals, which we then eat. **While the sale of milk containing antibiotics used in treating the increased rate of infection in cows that are administered BGH is prohibited, in a recent study it was found that 38% of milk contained illegal antibiotic residues. In addition, this milk is commonly contaminated with blood, pus and bacteria** resulting from a dramatically higher incidence of infection among cows treated with BGH. BGH milk is used in all of the commercially produced dairy products you might eat: butter, cheese, yogurt, ice cream, and even that latte you might sip every morning. It is the same milk served to your kids at school and used to make baby formula.

The routine use of BGH and antibiotics compounds an already serious problem with contamination by pesticides and chemicals concentrated in the milk. Amidst substantial and growing concern regarding the effects of non-therapeutic antibiotic use, the Union of Concerned Scientists in 2001 argued that the practice is harmful to humans, attributing the incidence of increasingly virulent strains of bacteria present in food to it.

Cattle and chickens were meant to feed on grass, which is full of chlorophyll, vitamins and minerals that are then transferred to us when we consume their meat, eggs and milk. What we get now is grain fed animals with lots of hormones, including estradiols, used to fatten them up more quickly so that they can get to market faster. **According to Samuel Epstein, a professor of environmental medicine at the University of Illinois at Chicago's School of Public Health and chairman of the Cancer Prevention Coalition, there is no safe level for its use. That, in fact, at any level, estradiols are carcinogenic.** In his book *The Politics of Cancer Revisited*, he cites studies that demonstrate substantial accumulations of the hormones in the muscle, organs and fatty tissue (including milk) of the animals. As a result, we ingest unknown quantities of those hormones every time we consume meat or milk products that were produced using them.

In addition, beginning in 1994, the dairy industry began using hormones in its milking cows to produce higher yields of milk. **The Bovine Growth Hormone (BGH) used in this practice causes an insulin-like growth factor (IGF-1) that survives the pasteurization process and is a growth factor for cancerous breast and colon cells.** BGH that is absorbed from the milk itself also produces IGF-1 directly in humans. Reportedly, Monsanto's own study data indicated elevated levels of IGF-1 in milk from BGH treated cows. A study of U.S. women published May 9, 1998 in *Lancet* showed a seven-fold increase in breast cancer among pre-menopausal women who had the highest levels of IGF-1 in their bodies. A study published in January 1998 in the journal *Science* linked higher levels of IGF-1 in men with a four-fold increase in prostate cancer. And, again, there is absolutely no safety data regarding children who consume substantially larger proportionate amounts of dairy products than adults. Children are also far more sensitive to the effects of hormones, even in minute amounts.

In 1989, the 15-nation European Union banned the import of most U.S. beef because of health concerns over cattle treated with growth hormones, allowing in only a limited quantity of the meat from the United States. Of course, the FDA and USDA are both quite cavalier about the use of hormones and antibiotics in livestock. In fact, they contend that there is no use for even providing testing of some substances any longer. The "experts" used to testify regarding the safety of the hormones in front of the World Trade Organization were not, in fact, scientific experts. What's more, nongovernmental agencies were not permitted to testify, resulting in a horribly imbalanced view of the issue. The FDA reduced pre-market testing requirements for BGH from 24 months using several hundred rats to 90 days using only 30 rats. Furthermore, the agency initially refused access to the data stating that it would "irreparably harm" Monsanto. **When Canadian scientists finally gained access to it in 1998, they found BGH linked with prostate and thyroid cancer in rats.** Still, the FDA approved it. Interesting, don't you think?

Used widely to fatten up livestock beginning in 1941, **it was determined by 1959 that diethylstilbestrol (DES) use in chicken and lambs produced sterility and breast growth in consumers**. It was subsequently banned for those markets, **but continued to be legal for use in cattle until 1979, twenty years after it was identified to be a health hazard.** This was also in spite of a clearly established link between in utero exposure and rare cancers in women identified by 1970. Given the number of problems we are beginning to see with respect to excessive hormone levels among girls, especially, we have great cause for concern regarding their use.

The FDA's spotty record on safety overall speaks for itself and it is one in which I believe the average consumer should take little faith in the absence of independent long-term data supporting the safety of the substances, particularly with respect to children. In addition, farmers have no obligation to inform us of their particular feeding practices, so you have no way of protecting yourself except to choose only organic meats and dairy products.

Furthermore, dangerous feeding practices have continued in the U.S. despite the development of mad cow disease. In 1989, meat and bone meal was banned in the European Union, but about 3 million tons are used each year in the United States to feed poultry and pork. Adding further insult to injury, it appears the FDA is not disposed to require labeling on cloned meat supply, either. What a bunch of jerks.

Pesticides

In its groundbreaking 1993 report *Pesticides in the Diets of Infants and Children*, the National Academy of Sciences (NAS) expressed enormous concern regarding the especially high vulnerability of infants and children to the effects of pesticides on their developing bodies. Furthermore, the NAS indicated its concern regarding the complete absence of any safety data representing the impact of pesticides on infants and children. While the Environmental Protection Agency (EPA) did nothing in response, Congress passed the Food Quality Protection Act of 1996 requiring the EPA ensure explicitly that pesticide residues were safe for children. Again, the EPA failed to take action and the FDA failed in its duty to enforce the requirements. As a result, on September 15, 2003, Massachusetts, New York, Connecticut and New Jersey filed suit against the EPA for failing to protect children from pesticides.

It was not as if the need for the EPA to take action was unclear. In addition to the 1993 NAS report, in 1998, the National Resources Defense Council reported that "the Scientific Advisory Panel to EPA's Office of Pesticide Programs . . . reviewed a study concluding that *every day*, **nine out of ten American children age six months through 5 years ingest organophosphate insecticides in their food. Organophosphates kill pests by poisoning the brain and nervous system. Yet the study further estimated that more than a million children each day eat an amount of these chemicals that exceeds the safe *adult* daily dose set by EPA**." In fact the CDC recently found that pesticide levels in children are on average twice those of adults. According to a study by the University of Washington, children who consume organic produce have *one-sixth* the level of pesticide residues in their urine as children who consume conventionally grown produce.

While commercially processed apples yield residues from an average of 2.4 pesticides, according to the Environmental Working Group, many fruits have four or five, with some apples testing positive for up to eight different pesticide residues. **Moreover, since the 1940s, crop losses from insect pests have doubled in spite of a *tenfold* increase in pesticide use.** Meanwhile the FDA maintains that the multitude of pesticides now in use are "safe". The agency also rigorously maintained that those now banned were safe until the very day their bans took effect.

Chemical Preservatives

Nitrites and nitrates are widely used in foods, many of which are popular among children. However, they are also known carcinogens. According to the Environmental Protection Agency (EPA), the chief danger with nitrates is that they are converted into nitrites during digestion, poisonous in humans and especially children and infants. The nitrites can combine with amines, a by-product of protein digestion, to form nitrosamines. According to the U.S. Surgeon general, nitrosamines are potent carcinogens and can cause malignant tumor growth over a long exposure period. The World Health Organization (WHO) reported that nitrosamines are also transplacentally carcinogenic in the second part of gestation.

Another danger associated with nitrites is that they can bond with hemoglobin, forming methemoglobin, which cannot carry oxygen. The result is oxygen deprivation. According to the EPA, young children are especially at risk from contact with nitrites. This is a particularly important point to remember because children are most likely to prefer the very foods that commonly contain chemical preservatives: namely, hot dogs, sausage, bacon, deli meat, canned meat, and reduced fat milk.

Avoid foods containing these two chemicals, especially if you are pregnant. High quality alternatives are readily available at stores specializing in organic foods. Even better, pasture fed versions are available through mail order.

What Should You Do?

If you don't choose to change your food sourcing habits simply for the health of it, try it just for the experience of having some of the most exquisite foods you have ever eaten. If you have never tried organic whole milk yogurt, for example, you don't know what you are missing. It is so good for you and is absolutely delicious. In addition, you may be interested to know that many high-end restaurants buy their meat from pasture fed sources. It is simply the best tasting meat you have ever had. Don't you and your family deserve the very best quality available?

An important part of altering our habits with respect to sourcing high quality foods is to adjust our expectations regarding the volume and availability of foods. High quality food is typically seasonal, especially in the colder regions. As a result, we have to do some real planning and preparation to compensate for those periods when the things we need to eat most are unavailable. For example, butter can be bought in bulk at summer's end and frozen for three to four months. The same goes for meats. Chances are, however, you will run out of some things before they become available again.

High quality foods are expensive. As demand increases, prices are likely to moderate somewhat, but I doubt it will ever be as cheap as the crap the big food companies are selling us now. It is also true that most of us eat more than we should. The average American currently eats about 200 calories more per day than they did 20 years ago while simultaneously becoming more sedentary. So there is a large proportion of the population that could easily cut back on their consumption by fifteen to twenty percent without the risk of going hungry. In addition, most of us waste a great deal of food by buying too much in the first place. We also eat out too much and rely too heavily on prepared foods, which tend to have all of the things we should avoid. If you take all of potential savings from these factors into consideration and then add those from a reduced need for over-the-counter medications, doctor's visits and prescription co-payments, you are likely to come out even on a dollar-for-dollar basis, at worst. If you further take into consideration the likelihood of increased productivity due to better health, you will surely wind up ahead of the game. In the end, we all pay one way or another when we cut corners.

If you are not fortunate enough to have a natural food store in your vicinity, there are some alternatives, particularly for dry goods. Many of the big chain grocery stores now offer organic foods to some extent. Another option is www.shopnatural.com, which offers an enormous variety of non-perishables in a wide range of sizes that can be shipped. At a price, of course. But it can work as a stop-gap measure, and if you plan wisely, you can minimize the shipping costs. There are also options for ordering organic produce online as well as raw milk aged cheeses.

Lastly, don't confuse "all natural" with healthy. I've noticed conventionally raised meats labeled this way and you should know that it has no relation whatsoever to what was done to the animal prior to slaughter. It still has all of the things you don't want in your meat. So don't be fooled by clever marketing.

I hope you find what follows to be practical suggestions for improving the quality of your food supply and, most especially, your health.

Educate yourself.

While it may seem self-evident, the truth is, we all tend to sit back and relax once we have found what we believe are reliable resources for making decisions. However, new discoveries are made continuously, and our lives change over time. So it is important to regularly re-examine your choices, just to be sure they continue to be the best ones for you. To the best of your ability, regularly research issues of diet, pesticides, chemicals, anything that is relevant to your well-being.

As I have mentioned throughout this piece, it is not meant to be an exhaustive review of data or a definitive piece on food quality. A simple *Google* search on the subjects of high fructose corn syrup, partially hydrogenated oils, and the other topics discussed in this book will provide all the information you could possibly want to ever see on the subjects. The site www.webmd.com can be somewhat useful on these subjects and for specific information on supplements and health issues. Also, Dr. Weston Price's *Nutrition and Physical Degeneration* contains a breathtaking review of his findings, including many photographs, which document the devastating effects of modern food processing practices. In her book *Nourishing Traditions*, Sally Fallon does a thorough job of reviewing in enormous detail changes that result from modern food processing techniques and provides a ton of recipes. I highly recommend it for people like me who don't really know where to start when increasing their protein intake. (Though, be forewarned that while it includes some great menu suggestions such as French Bean Salad with Marinated Grilled Swordfish, Bérnaise Sauce, Onions Chardonnay and Berry Sherbert, you will also find recipes for beef brains and other dishes that are somewhat beyond the interests of most people).

But, again, information is subject to interpretation. So if something just doesn't seem right to you, question it through a variety of resources until you feel you have a complete perspective for making informed decisions.

Start with the basics.

Have you ever looked at the recommended daily values on a nutrition label and wondered which category you fall under: the 2,000 calories or 2,500 calories? Well, here is a rule of thumb for determining just how much you should be eating every day. Calculate your baseline caloric needs by multiplying your *normal* weight by 12. You are the best judge of what a good weight is for you, so don't rely on arbitrary guidelines that define proper weight strictly by your height.

Then, consider how many more calories you might burn for specific activities and your lifestyle. Do you walk six blocks cross-town to work? Do you use the stairs regularly? Keep in mind that according to Marshall Brain's *How Stuff Works*, a person running a marathon burns only about 100 calories per mile. The average person might burn an extra 100 calories a day doing just regular stuff. Remember that it takes about 3,500 excess calories to add an extra pound to your waistline. While that may seem like a lot, a little treat every day can easily amount to five or more pounds a year, which can then quickly become 15 pounds in just a couple more.

Measuring fats, proteins and carbohydrates.

By weight, fat contains twice as many calories as carbohydrates and protein. Dr. Loren Cordain estimates that a 2400-calorie per day diet should include approximately

640 calories or 2.5 ounces (71 grams or 5 tablespoons) of **animal fat** including meats and dairy products. Each gram of fat equates to about 9 calories, which then translates into approximately 27% of total caloric intake.

In addition, **you need approximately 0.6 grams of protein per pound of normal body weight**. Protein is approximately four calories per gram. Remember that only animal protein is a source of complete essential amino acids, which are necessary for good cardiovascular health, proper cellular function and absorption of certain essential vitamins. Your body cannot produce them, so they must be consumed. While different vegetables in certain combinations can achieve the same outcome, they must be eaten simultaneously, which can be a pain in the neck. The best sources of highly nutritious protein are from organic pasture fed red meat (which contains as much as *80% less* saturated fat than grain fed red meat) and fatty fish.

The rest of your diet should consist of fresh fruits and vegetables. Carbohydrates from grains should be minimized, according to Dr. Cordain's research, and while he recognizes that it is nearly impossible to eliminate them completely from the average American's diet, one thing is clear: *carbohydrates belong at the top of the food pyramid, not the bottom*. The website www.atkins.com provides a carbohydrate counter to help consumers identify the net carbohydrates of commonly eaten foods as well as the protein and fat content. (*Note:* A recent survey found that most followers of the Atkins diet are consuming an average of 135 grams of refined carbohydrates, significantly above a recommended limit of 25 to 90 grams). Some people tolerate carbohydrates especially well, but you should still cut back to the extent that you continue to feel well and are able to maintain an appropriate weight. Make sure the carbohydrates you are eating are *whole* grains. A good barometer for choosing a grain product is that is should be chewy. You should actually have to work at masticating it. In addition, evidence suggests that it is not necessary to restrict carbs from fruits (except to the extent that you are drinking a lot of juice), vegetables and meats. The carbohydrate issue is about **grains**.

To see what a day's food consumption might look like under these guidelines, see Appendix A.

Evaluate what you are eating.

Read the labels on *everything* you buy and look out for high fructose corn syrup and partially hydrogenated oils. Find an organic substitute (organic foods do not use either of these in their preparation) or simply eliminate the item altogether from your diet. If you are thinking that all organic cookies and crackers taste gross, you haven't tried some of the newest ones. Barbara's Animal Cookies, for example, use real butter, whole wheat flour and fruit juice syrup instead of sugar to sweeten them and they are better tasting than any of the brand name animal cookies I've ever had. Newman's Own also makes an extensive line of delicious organic cookies. The reality is that you will not be able to avoid either HFCS or hydrogenated oils completely, but you must be vigilant in your efforts to avoid them. They are absolute garbage and will make you sick sooner or later.

Remember, however, that sweets are sweets and they should be consumed in great moderation. Two or three small cookies on occasion would be reasonable. No more.

Buy organic pasture fed meats and dairy products.

While you will most certainly experience sticker shock when you begin buying organic pasture fed products, as I did, you find that you tend to eat more appropriate amounts of food and waste less. One bonus is that you will reduce your risk of infection from virulent pathogens because the animals are not raised in an environment conducive to the growth of antibiotic resistant bacteria. But remember, not all pasture fed products are organic.

Meats. It only takes a few minutes to search for where to buy pasture fed meats on www.eatwild.com. There are listings by state if you would like to support pasture feeding in your area. There are also sites listed for on-line shopping. One is www.meadowraisedmeats.com where you can find beef, poultry, pork, lamb and veal. Best of all, you can also get delicious sausage and ham steaks that are salt cured and do not contain nitrites and nitrates. Don't allow yourself to be lulled into a false sense of security regarding the use of such chemical preservatives. The coop used to have chemical-free bacon and hot dogs, as well, but neither is currently available.

Another source is www.americangrassfedbeef.com, but it is limited to beef and you must buy in larger quantities. However, the site offers terrific variety with respect to cuts and is a more commercial operation with convenient payment and shipping options. You can also set up a regular monthly shipment.

Remember that pasture fed meat has a small fraction of the fat in comparison to grain fed meats (as little as 20%), and it simply melts in your mouth. Avoid cooking the meat at very high temperatures such as frying or grilling, as it produces elevated levels of carcinogens. Slow cooking at low temperatures preserves the nutrients and produces a delicious result. Stewing with the bone is best.

Raw milk. Search www.realmilk.com for raw organic pasture fed milk and other dairy products in your area. Apparently, the Royal British Family drinks it – and so should you. There are still some state restrictions on the sale of raw milk so it is not legally sold across the country. In places where it is, you usually have to buy it off the farm, but there are a few states where it can be sold in stores including California, Connecticut and Washington. If you live in a state that only allows it to be sold off the farm, you may be able to find or form a group to share regular trips to a regional dairy. If you get a large enough group together, you may be able to limit your responsibility to one or two trips a year as you rotate turns in the group. **Be sure to only source from a *licensed* dairy** that preferably uses Jersey or Guernsey cows, the *crème de la crème* of dairy cows.

Another option is cow-sharing if the sale of raw milk is prohibited in your state (make sure your cow has a negative tuberculosis test). If the sale of raw milk is prohibited in your state, write your local officials and demand that it be allowed. **All of the testing regarding the safety of milk that I have been able to find demonstrates that the track record of raw milk is, in fact, superior to pasteurized milk when obtained from a licensed dairy.**

An interesting historical note is that Dr. J. R. Crewe, of the Mayo Foundation, forerunner of the Mayo Clinic in Rochester, MN wrote extensively on his successful use of raw milk treatment for numerous illnesses.

Butter. Remember that commercial, "Give 'em all a little pat of butter"? Good advice, especially if cultured from organic, pasture fed raw milk sources. Don't overdo it, of course. Let common sense be your guide. If you are wondering if you are about to use too much, you probably are. Look on www.realmilk.com to see if you can find a source for pasture fed dairy products. One source that ships frozen pasture fed butter is Westminster Dairy. To order call 802.387.4412. The farm makes only a limited supply on a monthly basis. You can always buy in bulk and freeze the extra for up to four months. You get a better price, too. They also offer a number of aged and fresh cheeses. The hard cheeses are made from raw milk, but the fresh cheeses are made from organic pasteurized milk.

Eggs. They are typically seasonal in the colder regions, and if you cannot find an easy supply of them, other high omega-3 eggs will do. While not ideal (they are primarily grain, not pasture fed), it is a step in the right direction. Look for the words "free range" on the label, and chances are, the chickens are getting some grass in their diet. Most brands now label their eggs with omega-3 content due to increasing concern about chronically low levels in our diets.

Animal fat. You can freeze the fat from red meat cuts and easily shave off a few slices with a sharp knife for sautéing onions or other vegetables. I use salt pork when I make beans. Another easy and particularly yummy option is organic clarified butter, or ghee. It has a higher smoke point than regular butter, which reduces the risk that it will burn and become rancid. Make sure any animal fat you use for cooking is at least organic, if not from pasture fed sources. Small amounts of extra virgin olive oil are okay, too. Use only unrefined, cold-pressed oils that are kept in opaque packaging on a limited basis. Avoid using them for cooking, even canola, because they tend to become rancid and will make you sick over time.

Avoid pasteurized milk – even the organic kind.

While I am sure this may seem utterly preposterous to many people, the facts are overwhelming. It is true that milk "does a body good", but only if it is from a licensed dairy and *unpasteurized*. If you and/or your children are drinking pasteurized milk for the calcium, there are much better alternatives such as yogurt, organic pasture fed cheeses and dark leafy greens. **The enzymes in milk that make it possible to absorb its calcium are destroyed during pasteurization.** Even the vitamin D is of marginal value. An emulsified cod liver oil supplement is a superior alternative for vitamin D, however, you must take great care not to take too much. Go to www.mercola.com for details on how to supplement with vitamin D safely.

Pasteurized milk has been linked to diabetes - its amino acids are difficult to absorb and strain the pancreas. The cholesterol is oxidized, making it dangerous to your arteries. The fatty acids are rancid, creating free radicals that contribute to the development of cancer and heart disease. There is absolutely nothing redeeming about pasteurized milk. It is, in fact, *dangerous* to your health. You owe it to yourself to get to the truth of the matter and it is as simple as doing a *Google* search.

If you cook with milk and are unable to get it unpasteurized, buy organic and use it sparingly. Whatever you do, *don't* drink it by the glassful.

Buy only organic produce.

It is available almost everywhere now, and if you can't find it fresh, see what you can find frozen and adapt your recipes when necessary. Cascadian Farms produces a variety of high quality organic frozen fruits and vegetables. I find that frozen blueberries work quite well in pancakes, for example. Some areas have cooperatives through which it is possible to buy fresh organic produce in season. Delivery services are starting to pop up around some large cities, as well. It is also possible to buy organic produce online, but it is very expensive. Avoid conventional canned versions of fruits and vegetables for the same reasons you should avoid conventionally grown fresh ones.

Buy *only* fatty fish that is tested for contaminants.

This is extremely important for pregnant and nursing mothers. While enormously expensive, it is possible to find a limited supply of fatty fish that is free of contaminants. This includes farmed fish. In a January 2004 *Science* article, farmed salmon was found to contain significantly greater amounts of PCBs and dioxins than wild salmon. The good news is that organic fish farming is a brand-new, growing niche and will hopefully, depending on the type of feed used, be a near-term solution to the contamination problem.

Vital Choice is one brand of wild Alaskan salmon that claims to test free of contaminants is available on www.vitalchoice.com. If the prices are beyond your means, supplementation is the most cost-effective alternative. Fish oil does not typically contain contaminants, but you should only buy one that is tested. Carlson's is one brand. Be sure to store it correctly by refrigerating it so that it does not become rancid.

For those who live in the colder climates, a cod liver oil supplement is advisable during the winter months when the sun's intensity is too low to provide adequate exposure for optimal vitamin D. **The best option is cod liver oil that is naturally emulsified which not only reduces the fishy taste, but also makes the vitamin D more absorbable.** Cod liver oil typically contains high levels of vitamin A, as well, which can be problematic if you get too much of it. One brand that does not contain vitamin A and is tested for contaminants is Carlson's. Again, you must take care with respect to vitamin D supplementation so be sure to read up on www.mercola.com before beginning.

Both oils can be found on www.mercola.com and I can personally attest that the cod liver oil supplement is not at all offensive. I give it to my kids and they have no problem with it. The fish oil is lemon flavored and goes down reasonably well. My 5-year-old takes it straight and my 3-year-old eats it on his salad.

Use natural sweeteners.

Stevia is an *all natural* sweetener that tastes very similar to artificial ones. It is available in powdered and liquid forms and sold as a supplement at natural food and health food stores. Use in your coffee and other beverages in which you normally use sugar or artificial sweeteners. An extra bonus is that it is safe for diabetics and hypoglycemics.

Only use maple syrup. Don't touch that other "maple flavored" or "breakfast" syrup. It is junk in a bottle. Just look at the ingredients: high fructose corn syrup tops the list. It has no nutritional value whatsoever and it is, in fact, very *bad* for you. Maple syrup has calcium, iron and potassium in addition to being absolutely delicious.

Fresh whipped cream instead of sugar atop sautéed apples or fresh berries is a fabulous treat. It is easy to make whipped cream with a whisk or electric mixer and literally takes just a couple of minutes. Try to find organic, unpasteurized cream. Avoid the ultra pasteurized stuff, if you can.

Use organic cane sugar when baking. But remember, just because it is organic, does not mean it won't still make you fat if you eat too much. Ideally, you wouldn't have any refined sugar in your diet. But if you live in the real world, you should just try to minimize it.

Avoid fried foods and baked goods.

I'm sure you have heard this many times before with respect to fried foods. But it is good advice and cannot be overemphasized. Regularly eating fried foods will not only make you fat, they will also make you sick. High temperature cooking causes oils to become rancid and the result wreaks havoc on your body in the form of free radicals. Over time, they damage cells in ways that lead to cancer and heart disease. Keep your consumption of them to an absolute minimum and search for an alternative to them altogether.

You have probably never been told to avoid baked goods, however. They are, in truth, an insidious problem in our diets and Americans are much too fond of them. This includes cakes, cookies, bagels, doughnuts, muffins, pastries, breads and pies; just about anything you would find in your local supermarket bakeshop. The primary problem with commercially baked goods is the refined grains. The sugar only adds to the problem. Compounding issues are the consistent presence of hydrogenated oils and HFCS. Baked goods are just bad for you. They are not a treat. They are just plain bad food.

There are some organic alternatives for muffins and cookies that are less processed and do not contain hydrogenated oils or HFCS. But, again, even these should be consumed in great moderation.

Use sun dried sea salt instead of refined salt.

Use sea salt for seasoning and buy prepared foods that use sea salt instead of refined salt. It contains traces of marine life that are a readily available source of iodide that is sustained by the body over long periods of time, unlike the artificial iodide in refined salt that passes through the body quickly. It also contains other important minerals such as magnesium that are not present in refined salt and tastes better.

Avoid reduced fat milk and milk products.

This includes fresh yogurt and cheese. Several aspects of the processing create byproducts that have been shown to be toxic and/or carcinogenic. Besides, contrary to popular belief, you need the cholesterol and fat in whole milk to keep you healthy. As with everything, this means some, not a lot. Brown Cow whole milk yogurt is an excellent option as the milk comes from primarily grass fed Jersey cows, which has an unusually high protein content and nearly 6% butterfat. Although not certified organic, it uses only natural sweeteners (no refined sugars or corn syrup) and no additives or hormones are used. My understanding is that the cows receive minimal, if any, exposure to chemicals and pesticides. Many small dairy farms also produce fresh organic whole milk cheeses that are out of this world. Westminster Dairy, mentioned in the butter section, makes a decent variety. Be sure to ask when you inquire about raw milk in your area. Again, a *Google* search will find you whatever you need.

Start incorporating organ meats back into your diet, if you can.

This is especially important if you are finding it difficult to conceive or maintain a pregnancy. There is powerful evidence among native populations as well as large carnivorous mammals that organ meats are essential for good reproductive health. In particular, liver. Am I suggesting that you go out a buy a big old beef liver and cook it up with some onions? No. But what would you think to learn that traditional Bolognese sauce used chicken livers for flavor? Maybe you don't add a couple of whole livers to your sauce, but you could start by chopping up some of one and adding it to your recipe in small amounts. You can also do the same with beef liver. Drink a lovely glass of wine, take out the liver and mince a bit of it, or run it through a food processor, to combine in your favorite meatball recipe.

CAUTIONARY NOTE: It is important to remember that you *must* source organ meats carefully. Conventionally raised meats produce organs are loaded with toxins. Organic pasture fed is ideal, and organic is an acceptable alternative where pasture fed is unavailable.

Fish roe is also good for reproductive health.

Demand that your child's school stop serving processed and fried foods.

The rate of obesity among our children is horrific. It is truly criminal that they are being served foods that damage their health in an environment that is intended to be nurturing. The schools are funded by *your* tax money and you have every right, as well as an obligation, to ensure your children's good health. Do *not* tolerate the feeding of garbage to your kids at school. It should not be offered on the menu. Period.

Minimize your microwave use.

While most of us are heavily dependent on our microwaves for quickly reheating leftovers, etc., you should know that frequent use is putting your health at risk. According to a 1992 study published in *Pediatrics*, parents are advised not to heat formula or breastmilk in the microwave, because the process destroys some of the nutrients. Well, the same goes for regular food. Normal cooking heats a substance from without and the heat transfers into the food molecules through the cell membranes. Microwaving creates friction within the food molecules and their structures are torn apart and deformed (called structural isomerism) thus literally altering the molecular structure of the food itself.

In fact, a small controlled Swiss study conducted about ten years ago by Dr. Hans Hertel found statistically significant evidence that microwaves actually altered the food in such a way as to denature it and cause negative changes in human blood values once ingested. The negative changes included cholesterol levels (both LDL and HDL) and white blood cell counts, with cumulative effects. In other words, the study subjects demonstrated increasingly negative test results over time. However, the Swiss Association of Dealers for Electroapparatuses for Households and Industry quickly shut down the author of the study with a gag order so that the rest of us would not hear about it.

Furthermore, when you microwave food in plastic containers, the process causes the release of pthalates, which are used in the manufacture of plastics, and have estrogen-like properties. Once released, they bind with the food. Pthalates are believed to be a culprit in high estrogen levels among young girls.

While it is not unreasonable to use a microwave from time to time, take care not to use it routinely for cooking or heating food. One option I have found works nicely for reheating leftovers is to place the food in a metal colander on top of a saucepan with boiling water and cover. Literally, within just a few minutes, the food is nicely steamed and moist. Otherwise, heating directly in a pot is advisable. Always do so slowly and at low heat to best preserve the nutrients. While far less convenient than a microwave at first, once you are in the habit of using a stove, it really isn't so troublesome especially if you rinse the pots immediately after using them.

Ask your favorite restaurants if hydrogenated oils are used in their food.

Be specific. While some restaurants may not use hydrogenated oils on site in the preparation of your food, many restaurants use frozen prepared foods, which are often made with hydrogenated oils. This includes chicken tenders, bread, pizza, and cheese sticks as well as French fries. If they do, kindly ask that they find alternatives. Or write to the corporate office if it is a large chain.

Complain to the FDA.

The FDA's history with respect to assessing the safety of various substances used in our food supply is questionable, at best. Unfortunately, instead of being proactive, they are decidedly reactive to issues that arise with respect to food safety and routinely ignore the advice of expert panels it assembles to provide guidance. The reality is that the effects of many substances will only be known over long periods of time with routine exposure. And only once a body count starts to accumulate, does the agency finally take action as we have witnessed repeatedly over the years.

They work for *us*. If they can find the time to ban ephedra which is believed to have killed an estimated 100 people in recent years, they can certainly find the time to do something about trans fats when the FDA itself estimates more than 7,500 people become sick and 2,000 die from heart disease caused by *unlabeled* trans fats *every year*. This is not to mention requiring studies on "safe" amounts of pesticides, and other toxins on children. It is unconscionable that the agency has been so slow to take action on these matters. Their negligence would likely be considered criminal in the private sector. Furthermore, no one with an ounce of integrity would allow such serious matters to go unaddressed for such a ridiculous amount of time. It's their blasted *job* for crying out loud.

Thinking Ahead

One can't write about finding the best food sources without discussing the most important one to our long-term health and well-being: breastmilk. For some of you, this may be well off the focus of your interest, thus it is discussed here, at the end of the book. However, it is probably the single most important decision one can make with respect to their children. That goes for both men and women, alike, because successful breastfeeding is as dependent on the mother's commitment as the support of her family and friends. Once the opportunity is lost, it can never be recaptured.

There is much debate about breastfeeding and its value to an infant's overall health. The American Academy of Pediatrics (AAP) is now recommending at least one year, and the World Health Organization (WHO) recommends two. Despite a powerful body of evidence that children are immeasurably better off physically, emotionally and intellectually from sustained exclusive breastfeeding (i.e. no food until six months of age and no supplemental formula), rates are abysmally low in the United States. And the truth is, it is incredibly inconvenient to our go-go lifestyle.

My own experience tells me that a large part of the problem in initiating breastfeeding is misinformation from healthcare professionals themselves. All of the literature and guidance we get tells us that nursing should not be painful. If it is, it says, you are doing something wrong. Well, I am here to tell you that it can be *very* painful during the first couple of weeks. With all three of my children I, and every other new nursing mother that I have met, experienced at least some cracking, bleeding and, most certainly pain, early on. I can only imagine the number of mothers who have abandoned their efforts when they became convinced they couldn't do it properly as a result of these normal experiences.

Formula companies would also have you believe that what they make is just as good as breastmilk. Just watch the commercials depicting a mother holding a bottle to her infant's mouth as the strap on her nightgown falls off her shoulder. It somehow projects an image of full and complete nourishment and intimacy. Nice try, but nothing could be further from the truth.

In fact, **according to a recent independent analysis of more than 100 scientific studies, formula fed babies are twice as likely to die as breastfed babies.** A 2003 U.S. study found that formula-fed babies are *five times* as likely to die from Sudden Infant Death Syndrome (SIDS). In addition, a 1994 Finnish study found that the introduction of dairy products at an early age (i.e. cow's milk which is used in formula), increased a child's risk of developing type I diabetes. Formula fed babies have higher incidence of asthma, allergies and ear infections all of which can produce serious complications. The risks are real and cannot be underestimated.

Formula was originally designed for medical emergencies in which a mother could not provide the milk herself. Formula lacks many essential nutrients present in breastmilk including cholesterol, which is critical to brain development. It also lacks adequate saturated fat for proper nerve development and vitamin and mineral absorption. In addition, an absence of docosahexaenoic acid (DHA) contributes to the development of schizophrenia and has only recently been added on a limited basis. This is in spite of a 1996 campaign led by Frank Oski, retired Chairman of Pediatrics at Johns Hopkins University School of Medicine to which the FDA responded by refusing its approval. This is not to mention any of the benefits to a child from live antibodies present in breastmilk. Good medicine simply cannot compensate for their absence in infancy.

Formula companies would also have you believe that it is safer because of growing problems with environmental contaminants in breastmilk. However, not only have studies shown that breastmilk protects children from the effects of these contaminants, but the ingredients for formula are by no means free of chemical residues or hormones.

Even pediatricians seem to give little more than lip service to the AAP's own recommendation. They are quick to instruct new parents on the introduction of food as well as the use of supplemental formula. Furthermore, they seem better equipped to identify anomalies than help parents raise truly healthy babies. I am sure the threat of lawsuits has something to do with this, but it most certainly does not excuse it.

I also think that many people believe that since they were not breastfed exclusively for a sustained period of time and still wound up okay, that their children will be fine without it, too. The reality is, however, that like most things, the effects of not breastfeeding are realized over time. If you are over 35 years of age, think of how many of the kids you grew up with suffered from asthma, seasonal and food allergies, chronic ear infections or diabetes. Now consider how many children of friends and family that have any of those autoimmune problems. I imagine the number you can think of now is vastly greater than those with whom you grew up. And while exclusive breastfeeding of your child for a sustained period of time will probably not spare him or her from all potential illness, it will definitely swing the pendulum back in the right direction so that hopefully your grandchildren will be as healthy as you and your peers were growing up.

In the end, poor support and information available from our healthcare providers in addition to peer pressure to use formula make for a disastrous combination. Many American parents come away from the experience with very little appreciation for the unmatched benefits of sustained, exclusive breastfeeding. It is, by no means, *easy*, but the benefits are incontrovertible. Children who are fortunate enough to get off on the right foot in this respect have been shown to do measurably better physically, developmentally and academically as demonstrated by an 18-year study in New Zealand by John Horwood and David Fergusson. Don't your kids deserve the same leg up?

So, when you are on your way to having a baby, here are some very real and helpful hints to help you through.

Buy a tube of Lansinoh.

You can get it at most major drug stores and it comes in a lavender-colored tube. Make sure you have it with you when the baby is born. Initiate breastfeeding as soon after birth as possible, preferably within 30 minutes. Even when an emergency caesarean is performed, breastfeeding can easily begin within one hour of birth. Start using the Lansinoh right away, after the first and every feeding, to minimize cracking and bleeding. If you use it religiously, you may avoid having any pain at all. Don't buy the nonsense about using colostrum as a salve. It doesn't work.

If you can hear/see your baby swallowing during nursing, don't worry if he or she does not seem to have latched on "properly". As long as the baby is getting nourishment and it is not pinching you, ignore what you have been told about how it is supposed to look. You can also gently pull down the baby's bottom lip with your thumb to get its mouth in the phalanged position (it looks like a fish). This provides the best opportunity for the baby to get a good feeding and minimize your discomfort.

Keep the baby with you in your room.

In order to nurse on demand, you will need to see and hear your baby so that he or she does not reach a point of excitement and exhaustion from crying before they are able to nurse. It makes the enterprise far more difficult than if you can initiate the feeding immediately upon their interest. A new mother trying to nurse a hungry, crying newborn can be quite traumatic. Save yourself and your baby a tremendous amount of anxiety. If you are concerned about getting enough rest, you may find that you are more relaxed knowing that you are immediately available to the baby as soon as it needs you. Be sure to get a strong support network in tact before the birth so that you are able to catch up on your sleep during the day.

Also try and nap with your baby. The sound of its breathing can be very relaxing. And don't worry, you will not roll over on your baby if you are not taking medication or under the influence of drugs or alcohol. Just make sure there is enough space to prevent the baby from rolling off the bed. A rolled up towel can work well as a buffer between the baby and the edge. Just don't leave an infant alone in a full-size bed.

Delay introducing formula or food for as long as you possibly can.

Even if your child's pediatrician says it is okay to supplement, don't if you can avoid it. The only food your child needs for the first *six* months is breastmilk. It is only a matter of fashion to introduce any other foods before then, and it is *not* harmless to do so. Your infant's digestive system is not designed to absorb nutrients from cereal or any other food before six months of age, so even though it may be enriched, chances are that the baby is deriving very little, if any, nourishment from it. In addition, any cereal or fruit that it takes is in place of the vital nourishment it would otherwise get from breastmilk. In the end, you are substituting what is at best an inadequate source of nutrition for a perfect one. Furthermore, you are protecting your child from all manner of illness including ear infections, asthma, diabetes and obesity. Breastfed children also do better academically. Finally, weight gain should not be a primary consideration for introducing food or formula to your child unless there is a clear cut problem with the mother's milk supply.

A fat baby does not necessarily mean a healthy baby. The weight that a child gains should be appropriate to their height, frame and age. The source of a baby's weight gain is as important a consideration as an adult's. So if your child is gaining weight by consuming foods that are not truly good nourishment as we discussed earlier in this book, you are treading on dangerous territory with respect to his or her future health. It is not unusual for a breastfed child to develop low hemoglobin at around nine months when their iron stores are depleted. It should begin to improve as food is introduced. This is where ground, cooked liver can come in handy (*only* organic and/or pasture fed). Don't let yourself be pressured into cutting back on breastfeeding and substituting foods as this occurs.

Buy a double breast pump and start storing milk within the first month.

Your milk supply will be exceptional at this point and if you start pumping just once a day (preferably after your infant's morning feeding when your milk supply is at its peak of the day), you can build an ample inventory within a short period of time. This is especially important if you must return to work as it will spare you a great deal of stress as you attempt to meet your baby's needs while making the adjustment. Stress can reduce your milk supply and the last thing you need is to compound it by worrying that you cannot keep up with your infant's consumption. Be forewarned that it is by no means easy to continue your infant exclusively on breastmilk while working. I often wanted to give up with my first child, but a supportive La Leche League leader helped me through many days when I was ready to quit.

If, for some reason, you are unable to keep up with your child's need, breastfeeding even with a nominal supply of milk provides enormous benefits in more than one way. *Any* amount of milk provides antibodies, hormones and other important ingredients for your child's well-being. In addition, the act of nursing induces a state of awareness that is called "quiet alert" whereby your infant can more effectively process information from activities occurring around him or her than if not nursing. It facilitates neural connections that are critical to development and do not occur in its absence. Furthermore, it is impossible to know which ones are not made due to their subtle and complex nature. Nursing has also been shown to decrease the amount of pain an infant experiences. It is the ultimate source of comfort.

Even if you do not need to return to work, a small inventory of breastmilk will allow you periodic breaks to have dinner out or get an occasional haircut. You may have to pump while you are out, but once you have had some practice, it can usually be done in ten to fifteen minutes from start to finish if you have a double pump. Be sure to find one that can work with both batteries and a car adapter.

When you do introduce foods to your child, use only organic.

Earth's Best is a well-respected brand of organic baby foods that is carried by many conventional grocers. Any studies that have been done regarding the effects of pesticide residues or hormones on humans are with respect to adults only. It is simply not worth taking any chances. Just because you cannot see it, does NOT mean it is harmless. Furthermore, recall the current lawsuit against the EPA. Evidence suggests that children, and most especially, infants, are highly susceptible to the effects of chemicals and pesticides in conventionally grown and processed food. Also, while you are breastfeeding, consume as much of your diet from organic sources as possible. Again, it is not known how much of the residues you consume as well as the hormones in dairy and meat products are passed on to your child. Do not rationalize that formula is somehow safer. It is not. And it is not complete nutrition for your child and it can have very serious negative health consequences.

Visit The International Baby Food Action Network at www.ibfan.org to find a laundry list of studies showing that breastfeeding is superior to formula, including protection against E.coli bacteria, as well as higher motor activity and learning rates.

If you find that you are unable to breastfeed your child, homemade formula is a superior alternative to any commercially prepared one. The recipe can be found in Sally Fallon's *Nourishing Traditions* cookbook.

Closing Thoughts

I think as Americans, we tend to take the position that if a little of something is good, then a lot must be better. Deep down, we all know this is not true and in the end, we each have to take responsibility for our own choices and well-being. Know the true value of what you are eating. Then, eat what you require and no more.

That is not to say you should not enjoy your food. As I have mentioned good food can taste absolutely delicious. And, everyone deserves a little treat every now and then. But a treat should not be equated with something really "bad" for you. Fresh organic berries atop homemade ice cream from raw pasture fed milk, cream and eggs with a dollop of fresh whipped (pasture fed) cream is a true treat. While the sugar in the ice cream is not desirable, everything else will certainly contribute to your good health. So, when you think about allowing yourself something special, just remember that feeding your body well is about as special as you can get.

Furthermore, we have only ourselves to depend on for determining what is good and wholesome food. The FDA's track record is highly suspect. I don't pretend to have mastered all the challenges of feeding truly nourishing foods to my kids. They still want spaghetti every night, and rarely eat red meat. So, I sneak in a healthy dollop of butter in their tomato sauce and use it liberally in cooking their multi-grain pancakes, which I ferment overnight in raw milk. (I know this sounds bizarre, but the milk really doesn't go sour and the process makes the grains more digestible). I can only keep trying and hope that eventually they will come to enjoy all of the foods that I offer them. They are very interested to know that what I am feeding them will make them grow big and strong. They also take very seriously what I have told them about junk foods and can easily spot them amidst clever marketing. Verbally, my kids refute junk food, but I see they struggle with the fact that they really like to eat it from time to time. I hope my encouragement that I will always try to find good foods that they really like to eat helps stiffen their resolve against the things they know are bad for them.

For so long now, the "experts" have argued that organic foods are no healthier than conventionally grown and processed foods. I would like someone to explain to me how this logic works. Certainly people who eat organic foods still get sick. I don't think any reasonable person has ever argued that they don't. But the idea that eliminating pesticides, chemicals, hormones and antibiotics from our food supply does not somehow improve its quality is absurd on any level. Pesticides are there to *kill* things. The pesticides and chemical fertilizers used to grow crops have to stay on the plants to work. What washes off, goes into the soil that is there for the next planting. And the hormones and antibiotics that are injected into our meat supply don't just evaporate when the animal is slaughtered.

Finally, providing wholesome nourishment is not cheap or easy when compared to the processed foods marketed to today's families. For some of us, choosing high quality foods will mean sacrificing other comforts and habits we have come to depend on. But the evidence in incontrovertible. If you truly value your family's health, such choices will come more easily.

I hope you have found this book helpful. If it makes any difference in the way that you think about the food choices that you make, it will have been worthwhile.

Additional Sources

Statistical Brief #21: Trends in Outpatient Prescription Drug Utilization and Expenditures: 1997-2000 (online at www.meps.ahrq.gov/papers/st21/stat21)

Journal Report 01/01/2004 *New stats show heart disease still America's No. 1 killer, stroke No. 3* (online at www.americanheart.org/presenter)

The Truth About Saturated Fat (online at (www.mercola.com/2002/aug/17/saturated_fat1)

Office of Health Education, University of Pennsylvania, *The Top 10 Foods to Beware* (online at www.vpul.upenn.edu)

Eaton, SB et al. (1985) *Paleolithic Nutrition, a consideration of its nature and current implications.* N Engl J Med; 312:283-289.

Willett WC. *The dietary pyramid: does the foundation need repair?* Am J Clin Nutr. 1998;68: 218-219

The Paleolithic Diet and Its Modern Implications, An Interview with Loren Cordain, PhD, by Robert Crayhon, MS (online at www.mercola.com)

*Palmer, Linda, **The deadly influence of formula in America*** (online at www.naturalfamilyonline.com)

Gillette, Becky, *Doin' a body good?; studies link r-BGH-produced milk and increased cancer risk* (online at www.emagazine.com)

Quan, Richard, *Effects of Microwave Radiation on Anti-infective Factors in Human Milk*, Pediatrics (vol. 89, no. 4, April 1992)

Appendix A

Food	Protein g/serving	Fat g/serving	Carbs g/serving	Calories/ serving
Banana (small)	1	0.5	21.2	93
Nectarine	1.3	0.6	13.8	67
Whole Milk Yogurt (8 oz.)	7	9	25	210
Orange juice (8 oz.)	1.6	0.2	26.4	112
Cream of Tomato Soup	6.1	6	19.6	161
Turkey Breast (3 oz.)	21.3	6	0	162
Soft Hoagie Roll	7	4.5	30	200
Mayonnaise (1 tsp.)	0.1	3.7	0.1	33
Peach (medium)	0.7	0.1	8.9	42
Ground Chuck (6 oz.)	46.7	28.1	3.2	454
Slice Monterey Jack	7	8.6	0.2	106
Whole Wheat Bun	5	3.5	27	160
Mayonnaise (1 tsp.)	0.1	3.7	0.1	33
Ketchup (1 tbs.)	0.2	0.1	4	16
White Potato (0.5 cup)	1.1	0.1	13.9	66
Butter (1 tsp.)	0	3.8	0	34
Beer (12 oz)	1.1	0	12.5	146
Totals	**107.3**	**78.5**	**205.9**	**2095**

Protein from animals	*82.2*		*16%*
Fat from animals		*62.9*	*27%*
Carbs from grains			*69.5*	*15%*

Source: Values are from www.atkins.com

Notes:
1. The values indicated are for an inactive 180-lb. individual.
2. The serving sizes indicated are much smaller than you would normally find.
3. The yogurt referenced is for Brown Cow brand, which has a higher fat and protein content than most commercial brands.
4. Meat is not pasture fed.

Appendix B
A Shopper's Fieldguide

Ten Things to *Avoid*:
1. Baked goods
2. Anything fried
3. Pasteurized milk
4. Partially hydrogenated vegetable oil (in processed food)
5. High fructose corn syrup
6. Vegetable oil for cooking
7. Chemical preservatives
8. Reduced fat anything
9. Fatty fish not tested free of contaminants (i.e. tuna, mackerel, salmon)
10. Sugar

Ten Things to *Find*:
1. Raw organic milk, cream, butter, cheese, yogurt and eggs (preferably grass fed)
2. Organic grass fed meat (including organ meats)
3. Organic produce
4. Chewy, whole grain breads
5. Fatty fish tested free of contaminants
6. Sea salt
7. Fish and cod liver oil supplements tested free of contaminants
8. Natural sweeteners (i.e. maple syrup, raw honey, stevia)
9. Chlorella supplement
10. Sally Fallon's *Nourishing Traditions*

Appendix C
What Does Someone Raised On A Healthy Diet Look Like?

Those fortunate enough to be gestated and raised on a healthy diet share a number of distinguishing features. They include a broad, angular face with a thick skull formation capped by abundant thick hair, even into old age. In addition, they have deep and broadly set eye sockets, with wide noses and nostrils and prominent cheekbones, which allow for easy airflow. They have a low and broad dental arch with well-spaced white teeth, a square jaw, prominent chin and unoffensive breath even in the morning. Their bodies are well-proportioned with broad, square shoulders. Women have wide ribcages and waists with round, protruding pelvises to allow for short labor and easy childbirth. Their feet are also wide with splayed toes. If you happen to know anyone with such an appearance, chances are that person is rarely sick, incredibly resilient both physically and emotionally, and has optimism in spades regardless of their situation.

In contrast, even when a healthy individual adopts a modern diet, that person will produce offspring substantially different in appearance. Such children will have an elongated face with a thin skull formation and fine, thin hair. They have shallow eye sockets and flat cheekbones with narrow noses and pinched nostrils. Their dental arches are high and narrow, constricting airflow and trapping fluid in the sinuses. They have crowded, discolored and misshapen teeth, and small receding chins. Without regular brushing, their breath is offensive. Their shoulders are narrow and rounded. Women will have kidney-shaped pelvises and narrow waists, producing extended labor and difficult childbirth. They have narrow feet and crowded toes. Such a person is chronically sick with allergies and infections, has difficulty recovering, low energy and a generally poor outlook regardless of their situation.

About The Author

Patricia Negrón began her career as an equity analyst in 1992 in the asset management division of United States Trust Company of Boston. There she evaluated companies across all industries based on both qualitative and quantitative investment criteria, with an emphasis on sustainable practices. In 1996, she joined Boston investment bank Adams, Harkness & Hill where her research focused on the trademarked Healthy Living theme. While there, she published *Freshen Up Your Portfolio (1997)* and *Direct Selling: A Distribution Evolution (1999)* in addition to co-authoring several other related industry reports. In 1999, Patricia launched the financial advisory group at Breakaway Solutions, an Internet consulting firm, which she led until 2001. Currently, Patricia lives in Milton, Massachusetts with her husband and three boys.

CPSIA information can be obtained at www.ICGtesting.com
Printed in the USA
LVOW11s1913131215

466487LV00001B/6/P